A CONEY ISLAND
of the MIND

Books by Lawrence Ferlinghetti

A
CONEY ISLAND
of the
MIND

Poems by LAWRENCE
FERLINGHETTI

A NEW DIRECTIONS BOOK

CONTENTS

to K.

1
A CONEY ISLAND
of the MIND

The title of this book is taken from Henry Miller's INTO THE NIGHT LIFE. It is used out of context but expresses the way I felt about these poems when I wrote them — as if they were, taken together, a kind of Coney Island of the mind, a kind of circus of the soul.

1

In Goya's greatest scenes we seem to see
                              the people of the world
            exactly at the moment when
                they first attained the title of
                                    'suffering humanity'
            They writhe upon the page
                              in a veritable rage
                                    of adversity
              Heaped up
                    groaning with babies and bayonets
                                    under cement skies
              in an abstract landscape of blasted trees
                bent statues bats wings and beaks
                        slippery gibbets
                cadavers and carnivorous cocks
              and all the final hollering monsters
                    of the
                              'imagination of disaster'
              they are so bloody real
                        it is as if they really still existed

      And they do

          Only the landscape is changed

      They still are ranged along the roads
            plagued by legionaires
                              false windmills and demented roosters

      They are the same people
                              only further from home
            on freeways fifty lanes wide
                        on a concrete continent
                              spaced with bland billboards
                illustrating imbecile illusions of happiness

The scene shows fewer tumbrils
                     but more maimed citizens
                              in painted cars
          and they have strange license plates
       and engines
                  that devour America

2

Sailing thru the straits of Demos
we saw symbolic birds
shrieking over us
while eager eagles hovered
and elephants in bathtubs
floated past us out to sea
strumming bent mandolins
and bailing for old glory with their ears
while patriotic maidens
wearing paper poppies
and eating bonbons
ran along the shores
wailing after us
and while we lashed ourselves to masts
and stopt our ears with chewing gum
dying donkeys on high hills
sang low songs
and gay cows flew away
chanting Athenian anthems
as their pods turned to tulips
and heliocopters from Helios
flew over us
dropping free railway tickets
from Lost Angeles to Heaven
and promising Free Elections

                    So that
                              we set up mast and sail
on that swart ship once more
                              and so set forth once more
    forth upon the gobbly sea
                              loaded with liberated vestal virgins
and discus throwers reading Walden
                    but
                    shortly after reaching
                              the strange suburban shores
              of that great American
                              demi-democracy
              looked at each other
                              with a mild surprise
                    silent upon a peak
                              in Darien

3

The poet's eye obscenely seeing

sees the surface of the round world

        with its drunk rooftops

          and wooden oiseaux on clotheslines

         and its clay males and females

        with hot legs and rosebud breasts

        in rollaway beds

and its trees full of mysteries

and its Sunday parks and speechless statues

and its America

        with its ghost towns and empty Ellis Islands

and its surrealist landscape of

            mindless prairies

            supermarket suburbs

            steamheated cemeteries

            cinerama holy days

            and protesting cathedrals

a kissproof world of plastic toiletseats tampax and taxis

        drugged store cowboys and las vegas virgins

        disowned indians and cinemad matrons

        unroman senators and conscientious non-objectors

and all the other fatal shorn-up fragments

of the immigrant's dream come too true

      and mislaid

          among the sunbathers

4

In a surrealist year
                    of sandwichmen and sunbathers
                            dead sunflowers and live telephones
        house-broken politicos with party whips
        performed as usual
        in the rings of their sawdust circuses
        where tumblers and human cannonballs
                                filled the air like cries
                when some cool clown
                            pressed an inedible mushroom button
    and an inaudible Sunday bomb
                            fell down
catching the president at his prayers
                                on the 19th green

        O it was a spring
                        of fur leaves and cobalt flowers
        when cadillacs fell thru the trees like rain
                    drowning the meadows with madness
        while out of every imitation cloud
                            dropped myriad wingless crowds
                                of nutless nagasaki survivors
        And lost teacups
        full of our ashes
        floated by

5

Sometime during eternity
                              some guys show up
and one of them
                  who shows up real late
                                          is a kind of carpenter
        from some square-type place
                                      like Galilee
            and he starts wailing
                              and claiming he is hip
            to who made heaven
                                      and earth
                                              and that the cat
                  who really laid it on us
                                          is his Dad

        And moreover
            he adds
                    It's all writ down
                                on some scroll-type parchments
            which some henchmen
                              leave lying around the Dead Sea somewheres
            a long time ago
                              and which you won't even find
    for a coupla thousand years or so
                                      or at least for
        nineteen hundred and fortyseven
                                          of them
                    to be exact
                              and even then
            nobody really believes them
                                  or me
                                      for that matter

        You're hot
                they tell him

        And they cool him

        They stretch him on the Tree to cool

And everybody after that
                        is always making models
          of this Tree
                    with Him hung up
and always crooning His name
                    and calling Him to come down
          and sit in
                    on their combo
     as if he is the king cat
                         who's got to blow
     or they can't quite make it

     Only he don't come down
                    from His Tree

Him just hang there
               on His Tree
                         looking real Petered out
                    and real cool
                         and also
          according to a roundup
                    of late world news
     from the usual unreliable sources
                         real dead

6

They were putting up the statue
                of Saint Francis
            in front of the church
                of Saint Francis
                    in the city of San Francisco
        in a little side street
                    just off the Avenue
                            where no birds sang
        and the sun was coming up on time
                            in its usual fashion
                and just beginning to shine
                        on the statue of Saint Francis
                where no birds sang

And a lot of old Italians
                        were standing all around
            in the little side street
                        just off the Avenue
            watching the wily workers
                        who were hoisting up the statue
    with a chain and a crane
                        and other implements
And a lot of young reporters
                        in button-down clothes
        were taking down the words
                        of one young priest
        who was propping up the statue
                        with all his arguments

            And all the while
                        while no birds sang
                                any Saint Francis Passion
and while the lookers kept looking
                        up at Saint Francis
        with his arms outstretched
                        to the birds which weren't there

a very tall and very purely naked
                              young virgin
with very long and very straight
                         straw hair
and wearing only a very small
                            bird's nest
    in a very existential place
                 kept passing thru the crowd
                                      all the while
          and up and down the steps
                             in front of Saint Francis
       her eyes downcast all the while
                        and singing to herself

7

What could she say to the fantastic foolybear
and what could she say to brother
and what could she say
                        to the cat with future feet
and what could she say to mother
after that time that she lay lush
                             among the lolly flowers
      on that hot riverbank
         where ferns fell away in the broken air
               of the breath of her lover
   and birds went mad
                and threw themselves from trees
  to taste still hot upon the ground
                    the spilled sperm seed

8

In Golden Gate Park that day
                                   a man and his wife were coming along
        thru the enormous meadow
                           which was the meadow of the world
He was wearing green suspenders
                          and carrying an old beat-up flute
                                       in one hand
        while his wife had a bunch of grapes
                          which she kept handing out
                                       individually
                  to various squirrels
                                   as if each
                          were a little joke

    And then the two of them came on
                          thru the enormous meadow
which was the meadow of the world
                          and then
        at a very still spot where the trees dreamed
        and seemed to have been waiting thru all time
                                       for them
          they sat down together on the grass
                          without looking at each other
            and ate oranges
                      without looking at each other
                                   and put the peels
          in a basket which they seemed
                          to have brought for that purpose
              without looking at each other

    And then
              he took his shirt and undershirt off
          but kept his hat on
                      sideways
                          and without saying anything
          fell asleep under it
                          And his wife just sat there looking
    at the birds which flew about
        calling to each other

in the stilly air
as if they were questioning existence
or trying to recall something forgotten

But then finally
she too lay down flat
and just lay there looking up
at nothing
yet fingering the old flute
which nobody played
and finally looking over
at him
without any particular expression
except a certain awful look
of terrible depression

9

See
    it was like this when
                we waltz into this place
a couple of Papish cats
              is doing an Aztec two-step
And I says
       Dad let's cut
but then this dame
         comes up behind me see
              and says
        You and me could really exist
Wow I says
       Only the next day
      she has bad teeth
        and really hates
                poetry

10

I have not lain with beauty all my life
      telling over to myself
               its most rife charms

I have not lain with beauty all my life
           and lied with it as well
      telling over to myself
         how beauty never dies
    but lies apart
        among the aborigines
             of art
     and far above the battlefields
             of love

It is above all that
         oh yes
It sits upon the choicest of
        Church seats
up there where art directors meet
to choose the things for immortality
          And they have lain with beauty
     all their lives
        And they have fed on honeydew
  and drunk the wines of Paradise
          so that they know exactly how
   a thing of beauty is a joy
    forever and forever
         and how it never never
    quite can fade
       into a money-losing nothingness

Oh no I have not lain
                        on Beauty Rests like this
        afraid to rise at night
                            for fear that I might somehow miss
some movement beauty might have made

    Yet I have slept with beauty
                            in my own weird way
and I have made a hungry scene or two
                                with beauty in my bed
    and so spilled out another poem or two
        and so spilled out another poem or two
                            upon the Bosch-like world

11

The wounded wilderness of Morris Graves
    is not the same wild west
                the white man found
It is a land that Buddha came upon
                from a different direction
  It is a wild white nest
         in the true mad north
                 of introspection
     where 'falcons of the inner eye'
                 dive and die
       glimpsing in their dying fall
           all life's memory
             of existence
     and with grave chalk wing
           draw upon the leaded sky
  a thousand threaded images
          of flight

It is the night that is their 'native habitat'
  these 'spirit birds' with bled white wings
    these droves of plover
         bearded eagles
           blind birds singing
             in glass fields
  these moonmad swans and ecstatic ganders
                trapped egrets
        charcoal owls
            trotting turtle symbols
  these pink fish among mountains
          shrikes seeking to nest
    whitebone drones
        mating in air
   among hallucinary moons

And a masked bird fishing
                    in a golden stream
          and an ibis feeding
                    'on its own breast'

          and a stray Connemara Pooka
                              (life size)

And then those blown mute birds
                    bearing fish and paper messages
          between two streams
                    which are the twin streams
                              of oblivion
          wherein the imagination
                    turning upon itself
          with white electric vision
                    refinds itself still mad
               and unfed
                    among the hebrides

12

'One of those paintings that would not die'
    its warring image
                once conceived
    would not leave
              the leaded ground
  no matter how many times
                  he hounded it
                        into oblivion
Painting over it did no good
    It kept on coming through
                  the wood and canvas
  and as it came it cried at him
                  a terrible bedtime song
    wherein each bed a grave
                mined with unearthly alarmclocks
        hollered horribly
            for lovers and sleepers

13

Not like Dante

      discovering a <u>commedia</u>

                  upon the slopes of heaven

I would paint a different kind

         of Paradiso

in which the people would be naked

          as they always are

               in scenes like that

        because it is supposed to be

            a painting of their souls

but there would be no anxious angels telling them

     how heaven is

       the perfect picture of

           a monarchy

and there would be no fires burning

      in the hellish holes below

    in which I might have stepped

nor any altars in the sky except

            fountains of imagination

14

Don't let that horse
                    eat that violin

    cried Chagall's mother

                            But he
            kept right on
                        painting

And became famous

And kept on painting
                    The Horse With Violin In Mouth

And when he finally finished it
he jumped up upon the horse
                            and rode away
            waving the violin

And then with a low bow gave it
to the first naked nude he ran across

And there were no strings
                        attached

15

Constantly risking absurdity
                        and death
            whenever he performs
                        above the heads
                                    of his audience
        the poet like an acrobat
                        climbs on rime
                        to a high wire of his own making
and balancing on eyebeams
                        above a sea of faces
            paces his way
                        to the other side of day
    performing entrechats
                        and sleight-of-foot tricks
    and other high theatrics
                        and all without mistaking
            any thing
                        for what it may not be

        For he's the super realist
                        who must perforce perceive
            taut truth
                        before the taking of each stance or step
    in his supposed advance
                        toward that still higher perch
where Beauty stands and waits
                        with gravity
                        to start her death-defying leap

        And he
            a little charleychaplin man
                        who may or may not catch
            her fair eternal form
                        spreadeagled in the empty air
            of existence

16

Kafka's Castle stands above the world
like a last bastille
of the Mystery of Existence
Its blind approaches baffle us
Steep paths
plunge nowhere from it
Roads radiate into air
like the labyrinth wires
of a telephone central
thru which all calls are
infinitely untraceable
Up there
it is heavenly weather
Souls dance undressed
together
and like loiterers
on the fringes of a fair
we ogle the unobtainable
imagined mystery
Yet away around on the far side
like the stage door of a circus tent
is a wide wide vent in the battlements
where even elephants
waltz thru

17

This life is not a circus where
the shy performing dogs of love
                        look on
as time flicks out
                its tricky whip
                                to race us thru our paces
Yet gay parading floats drift by
                       decorated with gorgeous gussies in silk tights
                   and attended by moithering monkeys
                             make-believe monks
                           horny hiawathas
              and baboons astride tame tigers
                  with ladies inside
        while googly horns make merrygoround music
     and pantomimic pierrots castrate disaster
         with strange sad laughter
    and gory gorillas toss tender maidens heavenward
      while cakewalkers and carnie hustlers
          all gassed to the gills
             strike playbill poses
        and stagger after every
                     wheeling thing
   While still around the ring
                 lope the misshapen camels of lust
and all us Emmett Kelly clowns
                always making up imaginary scenes
with all our masks for faces
              even eat fake Last Suppers
                    at collapsible tables
       and mocking cross ourselves
                 in sawdust crosses

And yet gobble up at last
           to shrive our circus souls
     the also imaginary
              wafers of grace

18

Frightened
            by the sound of my own voice
    and by the sound of birds
                singing on hot wires
    in sunday sleep I see myself
                slaying sundry sinners and turkeys
loud dogs with sharp dead dugs
                and black knights in iron suits
        with Brooks labels
                and Yale locks upon the pants
    Yes
        and with penis erectus for spear
                I slay all old ladies
            making them young again
    with a touch of my sweet swaying sword
        retrouving them their maiden
                hoods and heads
                        ah yes
                    in flattering falsehoods of sleep

        we come we conquer all
                    but all the while
    real standard time ticks on
                and new bottled babies with real teeth
        devour our fantastic
                fictioned future

19

In woods where many rivers run
                        among the unbent hills
        and fields of our childhood
                        where ricks and rainbows mix in memory
although our 'fields' were streets
                        I see again those myriad mornings rise
    when every living thing
                        cast its shadow in eternity
        and all day long the light
                        like early morning
        with its sharp shadows shadowing
                                a paradise
            that I had hardly dreamed of
                        nor hardly knew to think
            of this unshaved today
                        with its derisive rooks
        that rise above dry trees
                        and caw and cry
    and question every other
                        spring and thing

20

The pennycandystore beyond the El
is where I first
                fell in love
                        with unreality
Jellybeans glowed in the semi-gloom
of that september afternoon
A cat upon the counter moved among
                        the licorice sticks
                and tootsie rolls
        and Oh Boy Gum

Outside the leaves were falling as they died

A wind had blown away the sun

A girl ran in
Her hair was rainy
Her breasts were breathless in the little room

Outside the leaves were falling
                and they cried
                        Too soon! too soon!

21

She loved to look at flowers
smell fruit
And the leaves had the look of loving

But halfass drunken sailors
staggered thru her sleep
scattering semen
over the virgin landscape

At a certain age
her heart put about
searching the lost shores

And heard the green birds singing
from the other side of silence

22

Johnny Nolan has a patch on his ass

Kids chase him
              thru screendoor summers

Thru the back streets
              of all my memories

Somewhere a man laments
                upon a violin

A doorstep baby cries
            and cries again
       like
        a
          ball
             bounced
               down steps

Which helps the afternoon arise again
to a moment of remembered hysteria

Johnny Nolan has a patch on his ass

Kids chase him

23

The Widder Fogliani
               otherwise known as Bella Donna
                    the Italian lady
                          of American distraction
the Widder Fogliani
                  was a merryoldsoul
        she had whiskers
                  on her soul
                       and her soul was a pussy
But she had a hard coming of it
                    that time I beat her
       at her own game
    which was painting moustaches
                     on statues
                in the Borghese gardens
            at three in the morning
and nobody the wiser
             if ever she gave
    some stray Cellini
             a free Christmas goose

24

We squat upon the beach of love
    among Picasso mandolins struck full of sand
        and buried catspaws that know no sphinx
        and picnic papers
            dead crabs' claws
            and starfish prints

We squat upon the beach of love
    among the beached mermaids
        with their bawling babies and bald husbands
        and homemade wooden animals
            with icecream spoons for feet
                which cannot walk or love
                    except to eat

We squat upon the brink of love
    and are secure as only squatters are
        among the puddled leavings
                    of salt sex's tides
        and the sweet semen rivulets
            and limp buried peckers
      in the sand's soft flesh

And still we laugh
    and still we run
        and still we throw ourselves
                upon love's boats
      but it is deeper
             and much later
                than we think
      and all goes down
        and all our lovebuoys fail us

And we drink and drown

25

Cast up
> the heart flops over
>> gasping 'Love'

a foolish fish which tries to draw
its breath from flesh of air

And no one there to hear its death
> among the sad bushes
where the world rushes by
> in a blather of asphalt and delay

26

That 'sensual phosphorescence
                         my youth delighted in'

  now lies almost behind me
                        like a land of dreams
              wherein an angel
                        of hot sleep
          dances like a diva
                        in strange veils
            thru which desire
                        looks and cries

And still she dances
                dances still

    and still she comes
                at me
                        with breathing breasts
          and secret lips

                and (ah)

                        bright eyes

27

Peacocks walked

under the night trees

in the lost moon
                        light

when I went out

                    looking for love

that night

A ring dove cooed in a cove

A cloche tolled twice

                        once for the birth

and once for the death

                    of love
                        that night

28

Dove sta amore
Where lies love
Dove sta amore
Here lies love
The ring dove love
In lyrical delight
Hear love's hillsong
Love's true willsong
Love's low plainsong
Too sweet painsong
In passages of night
Dove sta amore
Here lies love
The ring dove love
Dove sta amore
Here lies love

29

And that's the way it always is and that's the way
it always ends and the fire and the rose are one
and always the same scene and always the same
subject right from the beginning like in the Bible
or The Sun Also Rises which begins Robert Cohn
was middleweight boxing champion of his class
but later we lost our balls and there we go again
there we are again there's the same old theme
and scene again with all the citizens and all
the characters all working up to it right from
the first and it looks like all they ever think of
is doing It and it doesn't matter much with who
half the time but the other half it matters more
than anything O the sweet love fevers yes and
there's always complications like maybe she has
no eyes for him or him no eyes for her or her no
eyes for her or him no eyes for him or something
or other stands in the way like his mother or
her father or someone like that but they go right
on trying to get it all the time like in Shakespeare
or The Waste Land or Proust remembering his Things
Past or wherever And there they all are struggling
toward each other or after each other like those
marble maidens on that Grecian Urn or on any market
street or merrygoround around and around they go

all hunting love and half the hungry time not even
knowing just what is really eating them like Robin
walking in her Nightwood streets although it isn't
quite as simple as all that as if all she really
needed was a good fivecent cigar oh no and those
who have not hunted will not recognize the hunting
poise and then the hawks that hover where the
heart is hid and the hungry horses crying and
the stone angels and heaven and hell and Yerma
with her blind breasts under her dress and then
Christopher Columbus sailing off in search and
Rudolph Valentino and Juliet and Romeo and John
Barrymore and Anna Livia and Abie's Irish Rose
and so Goodnight Sweet Prince all over again
with everyone and everybody laughing and crying
along wherever night and day winter and summer
spring and tomorrow like Anna Karenina lost in
the snow and the cry of hunters in a great wood
and the soldiers coming and Freud and Ulysses
always on their hungry travels after the same
hot grail like King Arthur and his nighttime knights
and everybody wondering where and how it will all
end like in the movies or in some nightmaze novel
yes as in a nightmaze Yes I said Yes I will and he
called me his Andalusian rose and I said Yes my
heart was going like mad and that's the way Ulysses
ends as everything always ends when that hunting
cock of flesh at last cries out and has his glory
moment God and then comes tumbling down the sound

of axes in the wood and the trees falling and down
it goes the sweet cock's sword so wilting in the
fair flesh fields away alone at last and loved
and lost and found upon a riverbank along a
riverrun right where it all began and so begins again

2
ORAL MESSAGES

These seven poems were conceived specifically for jazz
accompaniment and as such should be considered as
spontaneously spoken "oral messages" rather than as
poems written for the printed page. As a result of
continued experimental reading with jazz, they are
still in a state of change. "Autobiography" and
"Junkman's Obbligato" are available on the Fantasy
LP recording No. 7002, "Poetry Readings in the
Cellar," which I made with Kenneth Rexroth and
the Cellar Jazz Quintet of San Francisco.

I AM WAITING

I am waiting for my case to come up
and I am waiting
for a rebirth of wonder
and I am waiting for someone
to really discover America
and wail
and I am waiting
for the discovery
of a new symbolic western frontier
and I am waiting
for the American Eagle
to really spread its wings
and straighten up and fly right
and I am waiting
for the Age of Anxiety
to drop dead
and I am waiting
for the war to be fought
which will make the world safe
for anarchy
and I am waiting
for the final withering away
of all governments
and I am perpetually awaiting
a rebirth of wonder

I am waiting for the Second Coming
and I am waiting
for a religious revival
to sweep thru the state of Arizona
and I am waiting
for the Grapes of Wrath to be stored
and I am waiting
for them to prove
that God is really American
and I am seriously waiting
for Billy Graham and Elvis Presley
to exchange roles seriously

and I am waiting
to see God on television
piped onto church altars
if only they can find
the right channel
to tune in on
and I am waiting
for the Last Supper to be served again
with a strange new appetizer
and I am perpetually awaiting
a rebirth of wonder

I am waiting for my number to be called
and I am waiting
for the living end
and I am waiting
for dad to come home
his pockets full
of irradiated silver dollars
and I am waiting
for the atomic tests to end
and I am waiting happily
for things to get much worse
before they improve
and I am waiting
for the Salvation Army to take over
and I am waiting
for the human crowd
to wander off a cliff somewhere
clutching its atomic umbrella
and I am waiting
for Ike to act
and I am waiting
for the meek to be blessed
and inherit the earth
without taxes
and I am waiting
for forests and animals
to reclaim the earth as theirs
and I am waiting
for a way to be devised
to destroy all nationalisms
without killing anybody

and I am waiting
for linnets and planets to fall like rain
and I am waiting for lovers and weepers
to lie down together again
in a new rebirth of wonder

I am waiting for the Great Divide to be crossed
and I am anxiously waiting
for the secret of eternal life to be discovered
by an obscure general practitioner
and save me forever from certain death
and I am waiting
for life to begin
and I am waiting
for the storms of life
to be over
and I am waiting
to set sail for happiness
and I am waiting
for a reconstructed Mayflower
to reach America
with its picture story and tv rights
sold in advance to the natives
and I am waiting
for the lost music to sound again
in the Lost Continent
in a new rebirth of wonder

I am waiting for the day
that maketh all things clear
and I am waiting
for Ole Man River
to just stop rolling along
past the country club
and I am waiting
for the deepest South
to just stop Reconstructing itself
in its own image
and I am waiting
for a sweet desegregated chariot
to swing low
and carry me back to Ole Virginie
and I am waiting
for Ole Virginie to discover

just why Darkies are born
and I am waiting
for God to lookout
from Lookout Mountain
and see the Ode to the Confederate Dead
as a real farce
and I am awaiting retribution
for what America did
to Tom Sawyer
and I am perpetually awaiting
a rebirth of wonder

I am waiting for Tom Swift to grow up
and I am waiting
for the American Boy
to take off Beauty's clothes
and get on top of her
and I am waiting
for Alice in Wonderland
to retransmit to me
her total dream of innocence
and I am waiting
for Childe Roland to come
to the final darkest tower
and I am waiting
for Aphrodite
to grow live arms
at a final disarmament conference
in a new rebirth of wonder

I am waiting
to get some intimations
of immortality
by recollecting my early childhood
and I am waiting
for the green mornings to come again
youth's dumb green fields come back again
and I am waiting
for some strains of unpremeditated art
to shake my typewriter
and I am waiting to write
the great indelible poem

and I am waiting
for the last long careless rapture
and I am perpetually waiting
for the fleeing lovers on the Grecian Urn
to catch each other up at last
and embrace
and I am awaiting
perpetually and forever
a renaissance of wonder

JUNKMAN'S OBBLIGATO

Let's go
Come on
Let's go
Empty out our pockets
and disappear.
Missing all our appointments
and turning up unshaven
years later
old cigarette papers
stuck to our pants
leaves in our hair.
Let us not
worry about the payments
anymore.
Let them come
and take it away
whatever it was
we were paying for.
And us with it.

Let us arise and go now
to where dogs do it
Over the Hill
where they keep the earthquakes
behind the city dumps
lost among gasmains and garbage.
Let us see the City Dumps
for what they are.
My country tears of thee.
Let us disappear
in automobile graveyards
and reappear years later
picking rags and newspapers
drying our drawers
on garbage fires
patches on our ass.
Do not bother
to say goodbye
to anyone.
Your missus will not miss us.

Let's go
smelling of sterno
where the benches are filled
with discarded Bowling Green statues
in the interior dark night
of the flowery bowery
our eyes watery
with the contemplation
of empty bottles of muscatel.
Let us recite from broken bibles
on streetcorners
Follow dogs on docks
Speak wild songs
Throw stones
Say anything
Blink at the sun and scratch
and stumble into silence
Diddle in doorways
Know whores thirdhand
after everyone else is finished
Stagger befuddled into East River sunsets
Sleep in phone booths
Puke in pawnshops
wailing for a winter overcoat.

Let us arise and go now
under the city
where ashcans roll
and reappear in putrid clothes
as the uncrowned underground kings
of subway men's rooms.
Let us feed the pigeons
at the City Hall
urging them to do their duty
in the Mayor's office.
Hurry up please it's time.
The end is coming.
Flash floods
Disasters in the sun
Dogs unleashed
Sister in the street
her brassiere backwards.

Let us arise and go now
into the interior dark night
of the soul's still bowery
and find ourselves anew
where subways stall and wait
under the River.
Cross over
into full puzzlement.
South Ferry will not run forever.
They are cutting out the Bay ferries
but it is still not too late
to get lost in Oakland.
Washington has not yet toppled
from his horse.
There is still time to goose him
and go
leaving our income tax form behind
and our waterproof wristwatch with it
staggering blind after alleycats
under Brooklyn's Bridge
blown statues in baggy pants
our tincan cries and garbage voices
trailing.
Junk for sale!

Let's cut out let's go
into the real interior of the country
where hockshops reign
mere unblind anarchy upon us.
The end is here
but golf goes on at Burning Tree.
It's raining it's pouring
The Ole Man is snoring.
Another flood is coming
though not the kind you think.
There is still time to sink
and think.
I wish to descend in society.
I wish to make like free.
Swing low sweet chariot.
Let us not wait for the cadillacs
to carry us triumphant
into the interior
waving at the natives

like roman senators in the provinces
wearing poet's laurels
on lighted brows.
Let us not wait for the write-up
on page one
of The New York Times Book Review
images of insane success
smiling from the photo.
By the time they print your picture
in Life Magazine
you will have become a negative anyway
a print with a glossy finish.
They will have come and gotten you
to be famous
and you still will not be free.
Goodbye I'm going.
I'm selling everything
and giving away the rest
to the Good Will Industries.
It will be dark out there
with the Salvation Army Band.
And the mind its own illumination.
Goodbye I'm walking out on the whole scene.
Close down the joint.
The system is all loused up.
Rome was never like this.
I'm tired of waiting for Godot.
I am going where turtles win
I am going
where conmen puke and die
Down the sad esplanades
of the official world.
Junk for sale!
My country tears of thee.

Let us go then you and I
leaving our neckties behind on lampposts
Take up the full beard
of walking anarchy
looking like Walt Whitman
a homemade bomb in the pocket.
I wish to descend in the social scale.
High society is low society.
I am a social climber

climbing downward
And the descent is difficult.
The Upper Middle Class Ideal
is for the birds
but the birds have no use for it
having their own kind of pecking order
based upon birdsong.
Pigeons on the grass alas.

Let us arise and go now
to the Isle of Manisfree.
Let loose the hogs of peace.
Hurry up please it's time.
Let us arise and go now
into the interior
of Foster's Cafeteria.
So long Emily Post.
So long
Lowell Thomas.
Goodbye Broadway.
Goodbye Herald Square.
Turn it off.
Confound the system.
Cancel all our leases.
Lose the War
without killing anybody.
Let horses scream
and ladies run
to flushless powderrooms.
The end has just begun.
I want to announce it.
Run don't walk
to the nearest exit.
The real earthquake is coming.
I can feel the building shake.
I am the refined type.
I cannot stand it.
I am going
where asses lie down
with customs collectors who call themselves
literary critics.
My tool is dusty.
My body hung up too long
in strange suspenders.

Get me a bright bandana
for a jockstrap.
Turn loose and we'll be off
where sports cars collapse
and the world begins again.
Hurry up please it's time.
It's time and a half
and there's the rub.
The thinkpad makes homeboys of us all.
Let us cut out
into stray eternity.
Somewhere the fields are full of larks.
Somewhere the land is swinging.
My country 'tis of thee
I'm singing.

Let us arise and go now
to the Isle of Manisfree
and live the true blue simple life
of wisdom and wonderment
where all things grow
straight up
aslant and singing
in the yellow sun
poppies out of cowpods
thinking angels out of turds.
I must arise and go now
to the Isle of Manisfree
way up behind the broken words
and woods of Arcady.

AUTOBIOGRAPHY

I am leading a quiet life
in Mike's Place every day
watching the champs
of the Dante Billiard Parlor
and the French pinball addicts.
I am leading a quiet life
on lower East Broadway.
I am an American.
I was an American boy.
I read the American Boy Magazine
and became a boy scout
in the suburbs.
I thought I was Tom Sawyer
catching crayfish in the Bronx River
and imagining the Mississippi.
I had a baseball mit
and an American Flyer bike.
I delivered the Woman's Home Companion
at five in the afternoon
or the Herald Trib
at five in the morning.
I still can hear the paper thump
on lost porches.
I had an unhappy childhood.
I saw Lindberg land.
I looked homeward
and saw no angel.
I got caught stealing pencils
from the Five and Ten Cent Store
the same month I made Eagle Scout.
I chopped trees for the CCC
and sat on them.
I landed in Normandy
in a rowboat that turned over.
I have seen the educated armies
on the beach at Dover.
I have seen Egyptian pilots in purple clouds
shopkeepers rolling up their blinds
at midday
potato salad and dandelions
at anarchist picnics.

I am reading 'Lorna Doone'
and a life of John Most
terror of the industrialist
a bomb on his desk at all times.
I have seen the garbagemen parade
in the Columbus Day Parade
behind the glib
farting trumpeters.
I have not been out to the Cloisters
in a long time
nor to the Tuileries
but I still keep thinking
of going.
I have seen the garbagemen parade
when it was snowing.
I have eaten hotdogs in ballparks.
I have heard the Gettysburg Address
and the Ginsberg Address.
I like it here
and I won't go back
where I came from.
I too have ridden boxcars boxcars boxcars.
I have travelled among unknown men.
I have been in Asia
with Noah in the Ark.
I was in India
when Rome was built.
I have been in the Manger
with an Ass.
I have seen the Eternal Distributor
from a White Hill
in South San Francisco
and the Laughing Woman at Loona Park
outside the Fun House
in a great rainstorm
still laughing.
I have heard the sound of revelry
by night.
I have wandered lonely
as a crowd.
I am leading a quiet life
outside of Mike's Place every day
watching the world walk by
in its curious shoes.

I once started out
to walk around the world
but ended up in Brooklyn.
That Bridge was too much for me.
I have engaged in silence
exile and cunning.
I flew too near the sun
and my wax wings fell off.
I am looking for my Old Man
whom I never knew.
I am looking for the Lost Leader
with whom I flew.
Young men should be explorers.
Home is where one starts from.
But Mother never told me
there'd be scenes like this.
Womb-weary
I rest
I have travelled.
I have seen goof city.
I have seen the mass mess.
I have heard Kid Ory cry.
I have heard a trombone preach.
I have heard Debussy
strained thru a sheet.
I have slept in a hundred islands
where books were trees.
I have heard the birds
that sound like bells.
I have worn grey flannel trousers
and walked upon the beach of hell.
I have dwelt in a hundred cities
where trees were books.
What subways what taxis what cafes!
What women with blind breasts
limbs lost among skyscrapers!
I have seen the statues of heroes
at carrefours.
Danton weeping at a metro entrance
Columbus in Barcelona
pointing Westward up the Ramblas
toward the American Express
Lincoln in his stony chair
And a great Stone Face

in North Dakota.
I know that Columbus
did not invent America.
I have heard a hundred housebroken Ezra Pounds.
They should all be freed.
It is long since I was a herdsman.
I am leading a quiet life
in Mike's Place every day
reading the Classified columns.
I have read the Reader's Digest
from cover to cover
and noted the close identification
of the United States and the Promised Land
where every coin is marked
In God We Trust
but the dollar bills do not have it
being gods unto themselves.
I read the Want Ads daily
looking for a stone a leaf
an unfound door.
I hear America singing
in the Yellow Pages.
One could never tell
the soul has its rages.
I read the papers every day
and hear humanity amiss
in the sad plethora of print.
I see where Walden Pond has been drained
to make an amusement park.
I see they're making Melville
eat his whale.
I see another war is coming
but I won't be there to fight it.
I have read the writing
on the outhouse wall.
I helped Kilroy write it.
I marched up Fifth Avenue
blowing on a bugle in a tight platoon
but hurried back to the Casbah
looking for my dog.
I see a similarity
between dogs and me.
Dogs are the true observers
walking up and down the world

thru the Molloy country.
I have walked down alleys
too narrow for Chryslers.
I have seen a hundred horseless milkwagons
in a vacant lot in Astoria.
Ben Shahn never painted them
but they're there
askew in Astoria.
I have heard the junkman's obbligato.
I have ridden superhighways
and believed the billboard's promises
Crossed the Jersey Flats
and seen the Cities of the Plain
And wallowed in the wilds of Westchester
with its roving bands of natives
in stationwagons.
I have seen them.
I am the man.
I was there.
I suffered
somewhat.
I am an American.
I have a passport.
I did not suffer in public.
And I'm too young to die.
I am a selfmade man.
And I have plans for the future.
I am in line
for a top job.
I may be moving on
to Detroit.
I am only temporarily
a tie salesman.
I am a good Joe.
I am an open book
to my boss.
I am a complete mystery
to my closest friends.
I am leading a quiet life
in Mike's Place every day
contemplating my navel.
I am a part
of the body's long madness.
I have wandered in various nightwoods.

I have leaned in drunken doorways.
I have written wild stories
without punctuation.
I am the man.
I was there.
I suffered
somewhat.
I have sat in an uneasy chair.
I am a tear of the sun.
I am a hill
where poets run.
I invented the alphabet
after watching the flight of cranes
who made letters with their legs.
I am a lake upon a plain.
I am a word
in a tree.
I am a hill of poetry.
I am a raid
on the inarticulate.
I have dreamt
that all my teeth fell out
but my tongue lived
to tell the tale.
For I am a still
of poetry.
I am a bank of song.
I am a playerpiano
in an abandoned casino
on a seaside esplanade
in a dense fog
still playing.
I see a similarity
between the Laughing Woman
and myself.
I have heard the sound of summer
in the rain.
I have seen girls on boardwalks
have complicated sensations.
I understand their hesitations.
I am a gatherer of fruit.
I have seen how kisses
cause euphoria.
I have risked enchantment.

I have seen the Virgin
in an appletree at Chartres
And Saint Joan burn
at the Bella Union.
I have seen giraffes in junglejims
their necks like love
wound around the iron circumstances
of the world.
I have seen the Venus Aphrodite
armless in her drafty corridor.
I have heard a siren sing
at One Fifth Avenue.
I have seen the White Goddess dancing
in the Rue des Beaux Arts
on the Fourteenth of July
and the Beautiful Dame Without Mercy
picking her nose in Chumley's.
She did not speak English.
She had yellow hair
and a hoarse voice
and no bird sang.
I am leading a quiet life
in Mike's Place every day
watching the pocket pool players
making the minestrone scene
wolfing the macaronis
and I have read somewhere
the Meaning of Existence
yet have forgotten
just exactly where.
But I am the man
And I'll be there.
And I may cause the lips
of those who are asleep
to speak.
And I may make my notebooks
into sheaves of grass.
And I may write my own
eponymous epitaph
instructing the horsemen
to pass.

DOG

The dog trots freely in the street
and sees reality
and the things he sees
are bigger than himself
and the things he sees
are his reality
Drunks in doorways
Moons on trees
The dog trots freely thru the street
and the things he sees
are smaller than himself
Fish on newsprint
Ants in holes
Chickens in Chinatown windows
their heads a block away
The dog trots freely in the street
and the things he smells
smell something like himself
The dog trots freely in the street
past puddles and babies
cats and cigars
poolrooms and policemen
He doesn't hate cops
He merely has no use for them
and he goes past them
and past the dead cows hung up whole
in front of the San Francisco Meat Market
He would rather eat a tender cow
than a tough policeman
though either might do
And he goes past the Romeo Ravioli Factory
and past Coit's Tower
and past Congressman Doyle
He's afraid of Coit's Tower
but he's not afraid of Congressman Doyle
although what he hears is very discouraging
very depressing
very absurd
to a sad young dog like himself
to a serious dog like himself

But he has his own free world to live in
His own fleas to eat
He will not be muzzled
Congressman Doyle is just another
fire hydrant
to him
The dog trots freely in the street
and has his own dog's life to live
and to think about
and to reflect upon
touching and tasting and testing everything
investigating everything
without benefit of perjury
a real realist
with a real tale to tell
and a real tail to tell it with
a real live
    barking
      democratic dog
engaged in real
     free enterprise
with something to say
     about ontology
something to say
    about reality
      and how to see it
       and how to hear it
with his head cocked sideways
      at streetcorners
as if he is just about to have
     his picture taken
      for Victor Records
    listening for
      His Master's Voice
   and looking
     like a living questionmark
      into the
      great gramaphone
      of puzzling existence
  with its wondrous hollow horn
   which always seems
  just about to spout forth
      some Victorious answer
      to everything

CHRIST CLIMBED DOWN

Christ climbed down
from His bare Tree
this year
and ran away to where
there were no rootless Christmas trees
hung with candycanes and breakable stars

Christ climbed down
from His bare Tree
this year
and ran away to where
there were no gilded Christmas trees
and no tinsel Christmas trees
and no tinfoil Christmas trees
and no pink plastic Christmas trees
and no gold Christmas trees
and no black Christmas trees
and no powderblue Christmas trees
hung with electric candles
and encircled by tin electric trains
and clever cornball relatives

Christ climbed down
from His bare Tree
this year
and ran away to where
no intrepid Bible salesmen
covered the territory
in two-tone cadillacs
and where no Sears Roebuck creches
complete with plastic babe in manger
arrived by parcel post
the babe by special delivery
and where no televised Wise Men
praised the Lord Calvert Whiskey

Christ climbed down
from His bare Tree
this year
and ran away to where
no fat handshaking stranger

in a red flannel suit
and a fake white beard
went around passing himself off
as some sort of North Pole saint
crossing the desert to Bethlehem
Pennsylvania
in a Volkswagon sled
drawn by rollicking Adirondack reindeer
with German names
and bearing sacks of Humble Gifts
from Saks Fifth Avenue
for everybody's imagined Christ child

Christ climbed down
from His bare Tree
this year
and ran away to where
no Bing Crosby carollers
groaned of a tight Christmas
and where no Radio City angels
iceskated wingless
thru a winter wonderland
into a jinglebell heaven
daily at 8:30
with Midnight Mass matinees

Christ climbed down
from His bare Tree
this year
and softly stole away into
some anonymous Mary's womb again
where in the darkest night
of everybody's anonymous soul
He awaits again
an unimaginable
and impossibly
Immaculate Reconception
the very craziest
of Second Comings

THE LONG STREET

The long street
which is the street of the world
passes around the world
filled with all the people of the world
not to mention all the voices
of all the people
that ever existed
Lovers and weepers
virgins and sleepers
spaghetti salesmen and sandwichmen
milkmen and orators
boneless bankers
brittle housewives
sheathed in nylon snobberies
deserts of advertising men
herds of high school fillies
crowds of collegians
all talking and talking
and walking around
or hanging out windows
to see what's doing
out in the world
where everything happens
sooner or later
if it happens at all
And the long street
which is the longest street
in all the world
but which isn't as long
as it seems
passes on
thru all the cities and all the scenes
down every alley
up every boulevard
thru every crossroads
thru red lights and green lights
cities in sunlight
continents in rain
hungry Hong Kongs
untillable Tuscaloosas
Oaklands of the soul

Dublins of the imagination
And the long street
rolls on around
like an enormous choochoo train
chugging around the world
with its bawling passengers
and babies and picnic baskets
and cats and dogs
and all of them wondering
just who is up
in the cab ahead
driving the train
if anybody
the train which runs around the world
like a world going round
all of them wondering
just what is up
if anything
and some of them leaning out
and peering ahead
and trying to catch
a look at the driver
in his one-eye cab
trying to see him
to glimpse his face
to catch his eye
as they whirl around a bend
but they never do
although once in a while
it looks as if
they're going to
And the street goes rocking on
the train goes bowling on
with its windows reaching up
its windows the windows
of all the buildings
in all the streets of the world
bowling along
thru the light of the world
thru the night of the world
with lanterns at crossings
lost lights flashing
crowds at carnivals
nightwood circuses

whorehouses and parliaments
forgotten fountains
cellar doors and unfound doors
figures in lamplight
pale idols dancing
as the world rocks on
But now we come
to the lonely part of the street
the part of the street
that goes around
the lonely part of the world
And this is not the place
that you change trains
for the Brighton Beach Express
This is not the place
that you do anything
This is the part of the world
where nothing's doing
where no one's doing
anything
where nobody's anywhere
nobody nowhere
except yourself
not even a mirror
to make you two
not a soul
except your own
maybe
and even that
not there
maybe
or not yours
maybe
because you're what's called
dead
you've reached your station

Descend

MEET MISS SUBWAYS

Meet Miss Subways
of 1957
See Miss Subways
of 1957
riding the Times Square Shuttle
back and forth
at four in the morning

Meet Miss Subways
of 1957
with fiftycentsize cotton plugs
in her flat black nose
shuttling back and forth
on the Times Square Shuttle
at four in the morning
and hanging on
to heaven's iron rings
with cut-up golden arms
a black weed in a black hand

You can meet Miss Subways
You can see Miss Subways
of 1957
wearing sad slacks
and matching handbag
and cruising thru the cars
and hanging on
with beat black arms
a black butt in a black hand

And the iron cars
shunting on forever
into death and darkness

o lost Ubangi

staggering thru
the 'successive ogives' of Hell
down Dante's final
fire escape

3
Poems from
PICTURES OF THE GONE WORLD
(1955)

This group of poems has been selected
from my first book, "Pictures of the Gone World,"
published in 1955 in the Pocket Poet Series
(City Lights Books, San Francisco 94133).

1

Away above a harborful
                    of caulkless houses
among the charley noble chimneypots
                    of a rooftop rigged with clotheslines
    a woman pastes up sails
                    upon the wind
  hanging out her morning sheets
                    with wooden pins
                O lovely mammal
                        her nearly naked teats
            throw taut shadows
                    when she stretches up
to hang at last the last of her
                    so white washed sins
        but it is wetly amorous
                        and winds itself about her
          clinging to her skin
                    So caught with arms upraised
      she tosses back her head
                    in voiceless laughter
    and in choiceless gesture then
                    shakes out gold hair

while in the reachless seascape spaces

                    between the blown white shrouds

    stand out the bright steamers

                    to kingdom come

2

Just as I used to say
                    love comes harder to the aged
because they've been running
                    on the same old rails too long
  and then when the sly switch comes along
                              they miss the turn
    and burn up the wrong rail while
                        the gay caboose goes flying
      and the steamengine driver don't recognize
                              them new electric horns
and the aged run out on the rusty spur
                            which ends up in
                    the dead grass where
    the rusty tincans and bedsprings and old razor
          blades and moldy mattresses
                                  lie
      and the rail breaks off dead
                        right there
      though the ties go on awhile
                          and the aged
say to themselves
              Well
                  this must be the place
          we were supposed to lie down

  And they do

              while the bright saloon careens along away
    on a high
          hilltop
                  its windows full of bluesky and lovers
      with flowers
                  their long hair streaming
                        and all of them laughing
          and waving and
                        whispering to each other
    and looking out and
                        wondering what that graveyard
      where the rails end
                      is

3

In hintertime Praxiteles
                laid about him with a golden maul
striking into stone
        his alabaster ideals
uttering all
      the sculptor's lexicon
           in visible syllables
    He cast bronze trees
         petrified a chameleon on one
    made stone doves
      fly
        His calipers measured bridges
    and lovers
       and certain other superhumans whom
he caught upon their dusty way
        to death

    They never reached it then

           You still can almost see
      their breath
        Their stone eyes staring
thru three thousand years
      allay our fears of aging

   although Praxiteles himself
        at twenty-eight lay dead

    for sculpture isn't for
        young men
  as Constantin Brancusi
      at a later hour
    said

4

In Paris in a loud dark winter

               when the sun was something in Provence

when I came upon the poetry

             of René Char

     I saw Vaucluse again

              in a summer of sauterelles

  its fountains full of petals

             and its river thrown down

through all the burnt places

            of that almond world

and the fields full of silence

           though the crickets sang

      with their legs

             And in the poet's plangent dream I saw

no Lorelei upon the Rhone

           nor angels debarked at Marseilles

but couples going nude into the sad water

             in the profound lasciviousness of spring

  in an algebra of lyricism

             which I am still deciphering

5

Sarolla's women in their picture hats
stretched upon his canvas beaches
beguiled the Spanish
Impressionists

And were they fraudulent pictures
of the world
the way the light played on them
creating illusions
of love?

I cannot help but think
that their 'reality'
was almost as real as
my memory of today

when the last sun hung on the hills
and I heard the day falling
like the gulls that fell
almost to land

while the last picnickers lay
and loved in the blowing yellow broom
resisted and resisting
tearing themselves apart

again

again

until the last hot hung climax
which could at last no longer be resisted
made them moan

And night's trees stood up

6

'Truth is not the secret of a few'
                                        yet
you would maybe think so
                        the way some
            librarians
    and cultural ambassadors and
                        especially museum directors
                                                act

        you'd think they had a corner
                                    on it
            the way they
                        walk around shaking
        their high heads and
                        looking as if they never
            went to the bath
                room or anything

        But I wouldn't blame them
    if I were you
            They say the Spiritual is best conceived
    in abstract terms
                and then too
        walking around in museums always makes me
            want to
                    'sit down'
            I always feel so
                            constipated
        in those
                high altitudes

7

Fortune
       has its cookies to give out

which is a good thing

       since it's been a long time since

    that summer in Brooklyn
when they closed off the street
    one hot day
    and the

          FIREMEN

            turned on their hoses
   and all the kids ran out in it

     in the middle of the street

   and there were

       maybe a couple dozen of us

          out there
with the water squirting up
       to the

       sky

        and all over
         us
   there was maybe only six of us
        kids altogether
    running around in our
       barefeet and birthday
   suits
    and I remember Molly but then

                the firemen stopped squirting their hoses
                    all of a sudden and went
                          back in
                      their firehouse
                          and
              started playing pinochle again
                  just as if nothing
                      had ever
                              happened
    while I remember Molly
                      looked at me and

        ran in

    because I guess really we were the only ones there

8

It was a face which darkness could kill
                              in an instant
   a face as easily hurt
                    by laughter or light

      'We think differently at night'
                              she told me once
   lying back languidly

                    And she would quote Cocteau

   'I feel there is an angel in me' she'd say
                    'whom I am constantly shocking'

      Then she would smile and look away
                light a cigarette for me
                                   sigh and rise
   and stretch
                her sweet anatomy

                         let fall a stocking

9

funny fantasies are never so real as oldstyle romances
where the hero has a heroine who has
long black braids and lets
nobody
kiss her ever
and everybody's trying all the time to
run away with her
and the hero is always drawing his
(sic) sword and
tilting at ginmills and
forever telling her he
loves her and has only honorable intentions and
honorable mentions
and no one ever beats him at
anything
but then finally one day
she who has always been so timid
offs with her glove and says
(though not in so many big words)
Let's lie down somewheres

baby

10

Terrible

a horse at night

standing hitched alone

in the still street

and whinnying

as if some sad nude astride him

had gripped hot legs on him

and sung

a sweet high hungry

single syllable

11

The world is a beautiful place
                              to be born into
if you don't mind happiness
                    not always being
                                    so very much fun
      if you don't mind a touch of hell
                         now and then
            just when everything is fine
                                 because even in heaven
                they don't sing
                      all the time

The world is a beautiful place
                              to be born into
if you don't mind some people dying
                                all the time
            or maybe only starving
                             some of the time
            which isn't half so bad
                         if it isn't you

Oh the world is a beautiful place
                              to be born into
         if you don't much mind
                      a few dead minds
            in the higher places
                        or a bomb or two
               now and then
                        in your upturned faces
      or such other improprieties
                           as our Name Brand society
                  is prey to
                         with its men of distinction
         and its men of extinction
                              and its priests
            and other patrolmen

                                        and its various segregations
              and congressional investigations
                                        and other constipations
                    that our fool flesh
                              is heir to

        Yes the world is the best place of all
                                        for a lot of such things as
                    making the fun scene
                              and making the love scene
        and making the sad scene
                              and singing low songs and having inspirations
              and walking around
                              looking at everything
                                        and smelling flowers
              and goosing statues
                              and even thinking
                                        and kissing people and
              making babies and wearing pants
                                        and waving hats and
                        dancing
                              and going swimming in rivers
                    on picnics
                              in the middle of the summer
              and just generally
                              'living it up'

        Yes
          but then right in the middle of it
                                        comes the smiling

                        mortician

12

Reading Yeats I do not think
                    of Ireland
but of midsummer New York
                    and of myself back then
        reading that copy I found
                    on the Thirdavenue El

        the El
            with its flyhung fans
        and its signs reading
                SPITTING IS FORBIDDEN

        the El
                careening thru its thirdstory world
        with its thirdstory people
                        in their thirdstory doors
        looking as if they had never heard
                            of the ground

            an old dame
                    watering her plant
        or a joker in a straw
                    putting a stickpin in his peppermint tie
    and looking just like he had nowhere to go
                            but coneyisland

        or an undershirted guy
                        rocking in his rocker
    watching the El pass by
                as if he expected it to be different
        each time

Reading Yeats I do not think
                         of Arcady
and of its woods which Yeats thought dead
                              I think instead
        of all the gone faces
                         getting off at midtown places
    with their hats and their jobs
        and of that lost book I had
                    with its blue cover and its white inside
where a pencilhand had written
                         HORSEMAN, PASS BY!

13

sweet and various the woodlark

who sings at the unbought gate

and yet how many

wild beasts
how many mad
in the civil thickets

Hölderlin
in his stone tower
or in that kind carpenter's house
at Tübingen

or then Rimbaud
his 'nightmare and logic'
a sophism of madness

But we have our own more recent
who also fatally assumed
that some direct connection
does exist between
language and reality
word and world

which is a laugh
if you ask me

I too have drunk and seen
the spider

INDEX OF TITLES AND FIRST LINES

New Directions Paperbooks

Ilangô Adigal, *Shilappadikaram.* NDP162.
Corrado Alvaro, *Revolt in Aspromonte.* NDP119.
Djuna Barnes, *Nightwood.* NDP98.
Charles Baudelaire, *Flowers of Evil.*† NDP71.
Paris Spleen. NDP294.
Eric Bentley, *Bernard Shaw.* NDP59.
Jorge Luis Borges, *Labyrinths.* NDP186.
Jean-François Bory, *Once Again.* NDP256.
Alain Bosquet, *Selected Poems.*† WPS4.
Paul Bowles, *The Sheltering Sky.* NDP158.
Kay Boyle, *Thirty Stories.* NDP62.
W. Bronk, *The World, the Worldless.* NDP157.
Buddha, *The Dhammapada.* NDP188.
Louis-Ferdinand Céline, *Guignol's Band.* NDP278.
Journey to the End of the Night. NDP84.
Blaise Cendrars, *Selected Writings.*† NDP203.
B-c. Chatterjee, *Krishnakanta's Will.* NDP120.
Jean Cocteau, *The Holy Terrors.* NDP212.
The Infernal Machine. NDP235.
Contemporary German Poetry.† (Anthology) NDP148.
Cid Corman, *Livingdying.* NDP289.
Gregory Corso, *Long Live Man.* NDP127.
Happy Birthday of Death. NDP86.
Edward Dahlberg, *Reader.* NDP246.
Because I Was Flesh. NDP227.
David Daiches, *Virginia Woolf.* (Revised) NDP96.
Osamu Dazai, *The Setting Sun.* NDP258.
Robert Duncan, *Roots and Branches,* NDP275.
Bending the Bow. NDP255.
Richard Eberhart, *Selected Poems.* NDP198.
Russell Edson, *The Very Thing That Happens.* NDP137.
Wm. Empson, *7 Types of Ambiguity.* NDP204.
Some Versions of Pastoral. NDP92.
Wm. Everson, *The Residual Years.* NDP263.
Lawrence Ferlinghetti, *Her.* NDP88.
A Coney Island of the Mind. NDP74.
Routines. NDP187.
The Secret Meaning of Things. NDP268.
Starting from San Francisco. NDP220.
Tyrannus Nix?. NDP288.
Unfair Arguments with Existence. NDP143.
Ronald Firbank, *Two Novels.* NDP128.
Dudley Fitts,
Poems from the Greek Anthology. NDP60.
F. Scott Fitzgerald, *The Crack-up.* NDP54.
Gustave Flaubert,
The Dictionary of Accepted Ideas. NDP230.
M. K. Gandhi, *Gandhi on Non-Violence.* (ed. Thomas Merton) NDP197.
André Gide, *Dostoevsky.* NDP100.
Goethe, *Faust,* Part I. (MacIntyre translation) NDP70.
Albert J. Guerard, *Thomas Hardy.* NDP185.

Guillevic, *Selected Poems.* NDP279.
James B. Hall, *Us He Devours.* NDP156.
Henry Hatfield, *Goethe.* NDP136.
Thomas Mann. (Revised Edition) NDP101.
John Hawkes, *The Cannibal.* NDP123.
The Lime Twig. NDP95.
Second Skin. NDP146.
The Beetle Leg. NDP239.
The Innocent Party. NDP238.
Lunar Landscapes. NDP274.
Hermann Hesse, *Siddhartha.* NDP65.
Edwin Honig, *García Lorca.* (Rev.) NDP102.
Christopher Isherwood, *The Berlin Stories.* NDP134.
Alfred Jarry, *Ubu Roi.* NDP105.
James Joyce, *Stephen Hero.* NDP133.
Franz Kafka, *Amerika.* NDP117.
Bob Kaufman,
Solitudes Crowded with Loneliness. NDP199.
Hugh Kenner, *Wyndham Lewis.* NDP167.
Lincoln Kirstein,
Rhymes & More Rhymes of a Pfc. NDP202.
P. Lal, translator, *Great Sanskrit Plays.* NDP142.
Tommaso Landolfi,
Gogol's Wife and Other Stories. NDP155.
Lautréamont, *Maldoror.* NDP207.
Denise Levertov, *O Taste and See.* NDP149.
The Jacob's Ladder. NDP112.
Relearning the Alphabet. NDP290.
The Sorrow Dance. NDP222.
With Eyes at the Back of Our Heads. NDP229.
Harry Levin, *James Joyce.* NDP87.
García Lorca, *Selected Poems.*† NDP114.
Three Tragedies. NDP52.
Five Plays. NDP232.
Carson McCullers, *The Member of the Wedding* (Playscript) NDP153.
Thomas Merton, *Selected Poems.* NDP85.
Cables to the Ace. NDP252.
Clement of Alexandria. Gift Ed. NDP173.
Emblems of a Season of Fury. NDP140.
Gandhi on Non-Violence. NDP197.
The Geography of Lograire. NDP283.
Original Child Bomb. NDP228.
Raids on the Unspeakable. NDP213.
The Way of Chuang Tzu. NDP276.
The Wisdom of the Desert. NDP295.
Zen and the Birds of Appetite. NDP261.
Henri Michaux, *Selected Writings.*† NDP264.
Henry Miller, *Big Sur & The Oranges of Hieronymus Bosch.* NDP161.
The Books in My Life. NDP280.
The Colossus of Maroussi. NDP75.
The Cosmological Eye. NDP109.
Henry Miller on Writing. NDP151.
The Henry Miller Reader. NDP269.
Remember to Remember. NDP111.
Smile at the Foot of the Ladder. NDP176.
Stand Still Like the Hummingbird. NDP236.
The Time of the Assassins. NDP115.
The Wisdom of the Heart. NDP94.

Y. Mishima, *Death in Midsummer*. NDP215.
  Confessions of a Mask. NDP253.
Eugenio Montale, *Selected Poems*.† NDP193.
Vladimir Nabokov, *Nikolai Gogol*. NDP78.
New Directions 17. (Anthology) NDP103.
New Directions 18. (Anthology) NDP163.
New Directions 19. (Anthology) NDP214.
New Directions 20. (Anthology) NDP248.
New Directions 21. (Anthology) NDP277.
New Directions 22. (Anthology) NDP291.
Charles Olson, *Selected Writings*. NDP231.
George Oppen, *The Materials*. NDP122.
  Of Being Numerous. NDP245.
  This In Which. NDP201.
Wilfred Owen, *Collected Poems*. NDP210.
Nicanor Parra,
  Poems and Antipoems.† NDP242.
Boris Pasternak, *Safe Conduct*. NDP77.
Kenneth Patchen, *Aflame and Afun of
  Walking Faces*. NDP292.
  Because It Is. NDP83.
  But Even So. NDP265.
  Collected Poems. NDP284.
  Doubleheader. NDP211.
  Hallelujah Anyway. NDP219.
  The Journal of Albion Moonlight. NDP99.
  Memoirs of a Shy Pornographer. NDP205.
  Selected Poems. NDP160.
  Sleepers Awake. NDP286.
Plays for a New Theater. (Anth.) NDP216.
Ezra Pound, *ABC of Reading*. NDP89.
  Classic Noh Theatre of Japan. NDP79.
  The Confucian Odes. NDP81.
  Confucius. NDP285.
  Confucius to Cummings. (Anth) NDP126.
  Guide to Kulchur. NDP257.
  Literary Essays. NDP250.
  Love Poems of Ancient Egypt. Gift Edition.
  NDP178.
  Pound/Joyce. NDP296.
  Selected Poems. NDP66.
  The Spirit of Romance. NDP266.
  Translations.† (Enlarged Edition) NDP145.
Carl Rakosi, *Amulet*. NDP234.
Raja Rao, *Kanthapura*. NDP224.
Herbert Read, *The Green Child*. NDP208.
Jesse Reichek, *Etcetera*. NDP196.
Kenneth Rexroth, *Assays*. NDP113.
  An Autobiographical Novel. NDP281.
  Bird in the Bush. NDP80
  Collected Shorter Poems. NDP243.
  100 Poems from the Chinese. NDP192.
  100 Poems from the Japanese.† NDP147.
Charles Reznikoff, *By the Waters of Manhattan*.
  NDP121.
  Testimony: The United States 1885–1890.
  NDP200.

Arthur Rimbaud, *Illuminations*.† NDP56.
  Season in Hell & Drunken Boat.† NDP97.
Saikaku Ihara, *The Life of an Amorous
  Woman*. NDP270.
Jean-Paul Sartre, *Baudelaire*. NDP233.
  Nausea. NDP82.
  The Wall (Intimacy). NDP272.
Delmore Schwartz, *Selected Poems*. NDP241.
Stevie Smith, *Selected Poems*. NDP159.
Gary Snyder, *The Back Country*. NDP249.
  Earth House Hold. NDP267.
Enid Starkie, *Arthur Rimbaud*. NDP254.
Stendhal, *Lucien Leuwen*.
  Book I: *The Green Huntsman*. NDP107.
  Book II: *The Telegraph*. NDP108.
Jules Supervielle, *Selected Writings*.† NDP209.
Dylan Thomas, *Adventures in the Skin Trade*.
  NDP183.
  A Child's Christmas in Wales. Gift Edition.
  NDP181.
  The Doctor and the Devils. NDP297.
  Portrait of the Artist as a Young Dog.
  NDP51.
  Quite Early One Morning. NDP90.
  Under Milk Wood. NDP73.
Lionel Trilling, *E. M. Forster*. NDP189.
Martin Turnell, *Art of French Fiction*. NDP251.
Paul Valéry, *Selected Writings*.† NDP184.
Vernon Watkins, *Selected Poems*. NDP221.
Nathanael West, *Miss Lonelyhearts &
  Day of the Locust*. NDP125.
George F. Whicher, tr.,
  The Goliard Poets.† NDP206.
J. Willett, *Theatre of Bertolt Brecht*. NDP244.
Tennessee Williams, *Hard Candy*. NDP225.
  Dragon Country. NDP287.
  The Glass Menagerie. NDP218.
  In the Winter of Cities. NDP154.
  One Arm & Other Stories. NDP237.
  The Roman Spring of Mrs. Stone. NDP271.
  27 Wagons Full of Cotton. NDP217.
William Carlos Williams,
  The William Carlos Williams Reader.
  NDP282.
  The Autobiography. NDP223.
  The Build-up. NDP259.
  The Farmers' Daughters. NDP106.
  In the American Grain. NDP53.
  In the Money. NDP240.
  Many Loves. NDP191.
  Paterson. Complete. NDP152.
  Pictures from Brueghel. NDP118.
  The Selected Essays. NDP273.
  Selected Poems. NDP131.
  White Mule. NDP226.
John D. Yohannan,
  Joseph and Potiphar's Wife. NDP262.

Complete descriptive catalog available free on request from
New Directions, 333 Sixth Avenue, New York 10014.   † Bilingual.